The Bloom

The Bloom

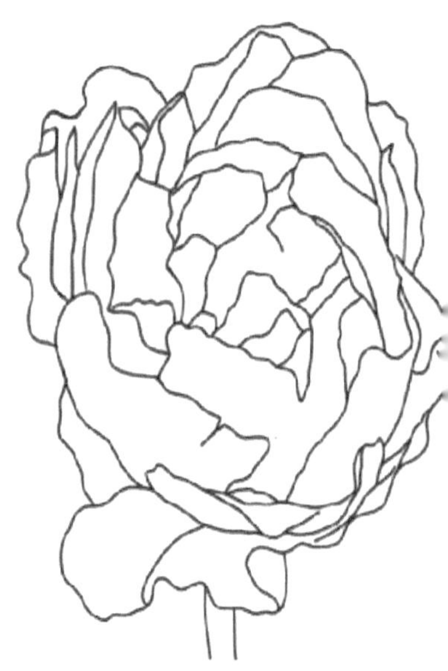

The Bloom

The Bloom

The Bloom

To

All that I was

All I am

And all I will be

The Bloom

The Bloom

Here in your hands dear reader,

Rest my thoughts,

The thoughts which screamed in the dead of
the night

Just to keep me awake

The thoughts of the afternoon which cried
themselves dry

Making my heart ache

And the thoughts of the morning aftermath

When the peace felt strange

The Bloom

The Bloom

Chapters

The Bloom

The Bloom

The Bloom

The Bloom

I made friends with the dark

With the moon and the stars

I made friends with silence

With peace and violence

I made friends with truth

With lies and with you

But in the morning when all left

It was despondency that helped me through

The Bloom

These days happiness feels borrowed

A loan which I'll need to repay

I can feel the debtors hovering around

Just waiting to strike

And ask for an interest I cannot afford to pay

Unless I let my heart end up as

Collateral damage

–––––––

The Bloom

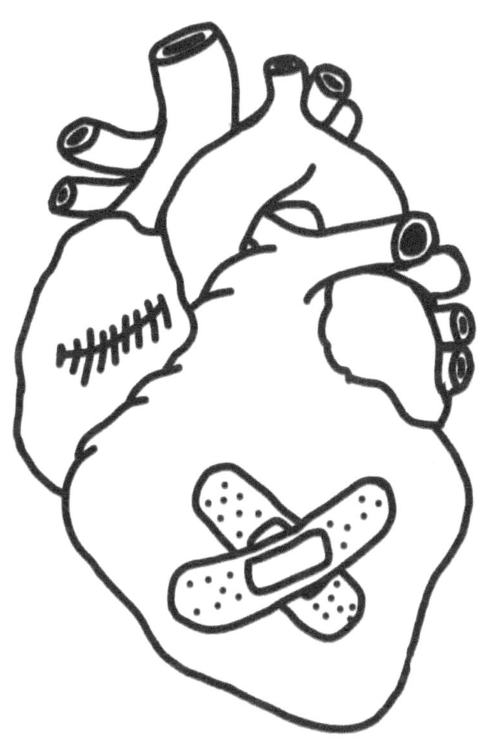

The Bloom

Glass houses are pretty

Glass houses make the outsiders think they
know all of that which goes on in the inside

Glass houses are best when you have
basements you want to hide

The musty underground where time seems
either too still or too fast

The one where after the entire day spent
above

You come down to know you can't run afar

The one which has the leftover shards

From when the house was built

The one where everyone stores their emotions
until it is time to bleed

The Bloom

I've started to forget the past

The memories are vanishing

The good as well as the bad

They are slipping from my fingers

Like they never existed at all

Tell me

Was I just chasing clouds?

– – – – – – – –

The Bloom

A reader's worst nightmare

Is being consumed by the thought

That you aren't good enough to be the main character

Even in your own book

-don't ask me why I write about fiction

———————

The Bloom

When the star fell and turned herself

Into dust

Did the moon wish on it?

Hoping for someone

The Bloom

What if they call my bluff?

And know

That

All

Is

Just

For

Show

The queen of hearts was long lost before I
could choose

I've dealt all my cards, I can't afford to lose

— — — — — — — —

The Bloom

The Bloom

The more

People I

Meet

The more

Alien

I feel

- - - - - - -

The Bloom

In this world I've found nothing more faker

Than to be a lover

And a heartbreaker

Both of which together

As if you can give

And still be the taker

— — — — — — —

The Bloom

Expectations are what makes me burn

Expectations are what make me run

Expectations are what make me feel

Expectations are what make me, me

For I am a stick of dynamite with a matchstick I
hand

Hoping you'd know

Thinking you'd understand

– – – – – – – –

The Bloom

Can we uncomplicate the complicated

Can we go back in time

Maybe picture perfect lies

Are better than silent cries

Maybe it can be undone

Maybe it wasn't true

Maybe 3+3 make 10

And maybe in the end it's you

The Bloom

If the world was on fire

I would still try to water down the flame

The way I do

When I hear your name

Because it's either the scorching forest fire

Or the drowning rain

_ _ _ _ _ _ _

The Bloom

I try to hold on

I always do

But sometimes

The edge gives in and crumbles

It doesn't matter that I tried my best

Because the circumstance wasn't my supporter

And neither was fate.

— — — — — — —

The Bloom

Sometimes I wonder

Do I speak my truth

Or

Do I lie as a favour

Do my words hurt someone

Or

Do they not matter

Do I act like I think I do

Or

Do I imagine all of it as true

Do I know what I am doing

Or

Do I just act unbecoming

— — — — — — —

The Bloom

Sometimes

I'm met with this

Crazy fearful thought

What if I never get over you at all?

— — — — — — —

The Bloom

How was I supposed to know

You were a prison I had to escape when I
couldn't see a prison at all

Was it made of glass or was I too blind

Is that why I jumped without seeing where I
would fall

How can a prisoner need escaping

When in her mind she's no prisoner

And how can a captivator sympathise

When justification is a loaded gun ready to fire

– – – – – – –

The Bloom

The Bloom

You asked for forgiveness

But she didn't

You gave reason

But she didn't

You presented alibis

But she didn't

You left me plagued with memories

But she (my heart) who took the blame

Couldn't

– – – – – – –

The Bloom

I wish I had a name to write

Instead of 'dear diary'

To deceive me into believing

That someone somewhere would like to hear

All that I would say

To deceive me into believing

That I can find a home

In things beyond the inanimate world

-if a house is not a home

Then where do I go

_ _ _ _ _ _ _

The Bloom

Yesterday I was your moon

Today I'm a star

Burning as bright as I can just to be seen by you
even if it's only from afar

Only for a moment

Only to be forgotten

Only to be loved

In a past that's rotten

– – – – – – –

The Bloom

The Bloom

Romance is not dead

For it was never alive

Just a figment of our imagination

Helping us survive

Making us think we were not alone

Painting the illusion that we had a home

Where we could be free from judgement

It's all fool's gold

Under all the honeyed attachment

‒ ‒ ‒ ‒ ‒ ‒ ‒

The Bloom

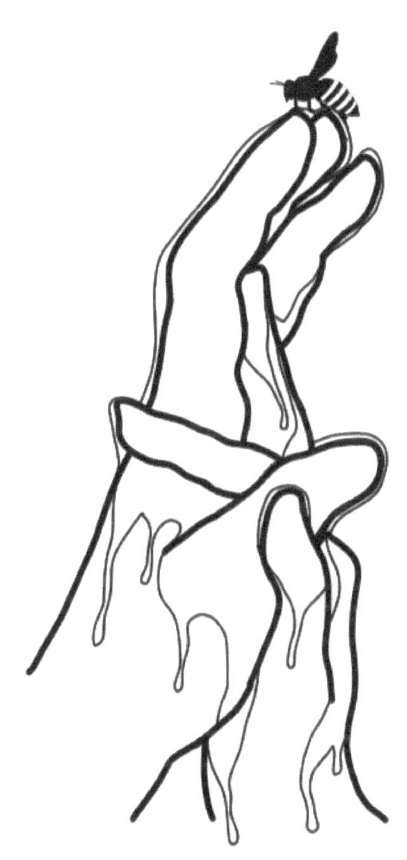

The Bloom

I would just smile

Smile through the pain

You would just smile

Smile through the train wreck you caused

And you still wanted it all

My blood, my bruise, my song

— — — — — — —

The Bloom

I hate it when people wish they were someone
else

As if you knew all the pain they felt

And still wish to go through that hell

I hate it when people wish they were someone
else

Not knowing that all that person wants is for
her to change

\- - - - - - -

The Bloom

You

My darling

Created this world which was

Pieces of us strung together in a cocoon of
warmth

But when the time came for you to spread your
wings

You tore through this cocoon

And flew away

Leaving me right here

Without the warmth of home

Or a way to go

Back

To where I came from

The Bloom

The Bloom

I miss being sad

It seemed like the only constant I had

For a while.

– – – – – – –

The Bloom

The Bloom

Winter

The Bloom

The Bloom

I'm not in denial

The truth is what it is

It's right there for me to see, hear, feel

It's right there to make me hurt, angry, bleed

It's right there, scarring me deep underneath

I'm not in denial

Just clinging on to the last bit of hope

That this is just a dream

———————

The Bloom

Sometimes

You can't untangle it

Without

Letting go

_ _ _ _ _ _ _

The Bloom

The Bloom

I was never the art

I never sat still in a place

To see myself through the eyes of someone

I never heard myself in the words of someone

I never was the object of such deep fascination

That in the hope of getting me out of their
head

Someone immortalized me onto pages, into
words

For I was never the art

Neither was I the artist

No one would stay long enough for me to paint
them

No one would hear long enough for me to sing
them

No one would become my all if their departure
was known to me even before they were

The Bloom

I was never the artist

I was never the art

Just an admirer from afar

— — — — — — —

The Bloom

Maybe it was better when I knew less

When I looked at everything

Through rose tinted glasses

At least then I was happier and not

Blue

The way I am when I think of all the truths

Maybe it was better when I knew less

Because then I could chalk it up to ignorance
and not stress

Maybe it was better I knew less

When life seemed full of possibilities and zest

– – – – – – – –

The Bloom

If all that I've learnt

And all that I've lost

Made me someone who never thought of you
at all

Then why does all that I've loved

And all that I've got

End up leading me to you somehow

_ _ _ _ _ _ _

The Bloom

A broken teacup

Can never be the way it was

No matter how beautiful it was before

The cracks will show

And that is the truth

The cracks are here to stay

But that doesn't mean that the cracks can't add

To a new kind of beauty

————————

The Bloom

The Bloom

I didn't make it to the bed

The gravity stuck my bones to the floor

Like ash to my lungs from when you burnt

The house I built where I could be myself

A few words crumble the pillars and support as
if they were made of your promises

I didn't make it to bed today but I'm glad that I
could atleast fall asleep

Eventhough it was on the cold floor of the
living room

Breathing the fresh new paint

-rebuilding takes time

———————

The Bloom

The Bloom

My love for you is 6 feet underground

But its ghost still haunts me

It was an open casket but you never came to see

You handed me the knife but never told me what to do

So plunged it in the chest of what I felt for you

Hoping it would go away and I guess it did

But in the matter of heart, realism doesn't exist

So every once in a while I hear footsteps tiptoeing

When I'm wishing it's not my love for you that haunting

Me

The Bloom

The Bloom

I miss looking at the stars and thinking you
were looking at them too

But I think I miss the constellations more than I
miss you

I miss smelling flowers, the ones you got me
too

But I think I miss the smell more than I miss
you

I miss holding you close and how you held me
too

But think I miss the warmth more than I miss
you

And I miss knowing that I had you

But I know that I miss having someone more
than I miss having you

— — — — — — —

The Bloom

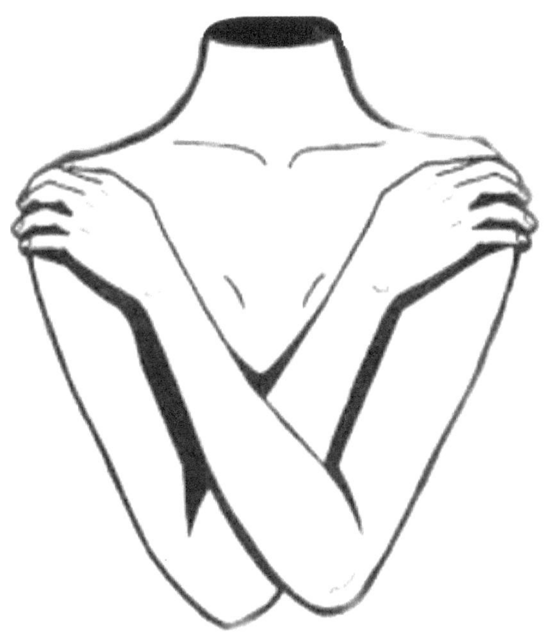

The Bloom

I'm starting to understand

The bitter smiles our parents had

When we would dream of growing up and
living all the childish fantasies

That we concocted in our minds

———————

The Bloom

I wonder how the poets do it

I wonder how they express this love in words

How can they fit the universe on pages

Only for the pages to burn

Is it easy for them because they feel

Or do they feel for the words to bleed

So that every other emotion pales in
comparison

To the blood that runs clean

– – – – – – – –

The Bloom

Do I know myself ?

-yes I do

Do I love myself?

-knowing, tell me not to

Do I listen to my head then?

-even humans make mistakes

Then is loving me the mistake you made?

But this is not about you

This is about me

Because if I loved you

It meant I loved me

Then why is it so hard for me to believe

That I'm enough to get me wherever I need

Is loving myself arrogant

The Bloom

-why would it be

Isn't that what you always told me?

-you're going back to the past

I'm trying, please believe

-the past has left you and it's time

For you too to leave

— — — — — — —

The Bloom

I tried to draw the perfect cloud in the sand

One which was shaped the way I was told
clouds should be shaped

But this one looked nothing like the one drawn
in the sky

The imperfection above was prettier that the
thought perfection below

It was real

Not fabricated by imagination or expectations

It was what we saw everyday but never learnt
to appreciate

Soon the sea roared in and washed the slate of
sand clean

Perfect for me to start drawing a flower

The thorns prickling before they were taken by
the sea

____

The Bloom

Am I still a sinner

If

I am sorry

Are you still telling the truth

When you ask me not to worry

Is the world flat

If I see the edge

Am I still the person I was

Even if I have to pretend

I am

– – – – – – –

The Bloom

Trust me when I say

I really tried

But sometimes I wonder

If that's what drove you to say

Goodbye

I wonder if there had been a way for me to
know

That me loving you so

Was what made you let go

– – – – – – –

The Bloom

I didn't think I would make it past those days

I didn't want to

But here I am

Fighting everything

That I wanted to give in to

— — — — — — —

The Bloom

It doesn't hurt anymore the way hurt easily fell
from your lips

It doesn't hurt anymore the way I tried to save
this

It doesn't hurt anymore how you would share
the blame

And it doesn't hurt anymore when I think of
the shame I felt

It doesn't hurt but it did leave a scar

A jagged battle mark

Like the wine stain on my carpet

But it's alright because I'll just flip it like a
moment

To the otherside where the past is left behind
me

Where the past is long gone in a distant
memory

The Bloom

Where the past is a lesson that I learn from

Where the past is the only place you and I
could together belong

– – – – – – – –

The Bloom

What should I make of the fact

That the start of my growth

Was the end of ours

The moment when you realised

That I had changed

For the better

Was the moment you wanted me to stay the same

Forever

Forever the person in pieces you met

Forever the person whose independence was fake

Forever the past

Forever your muse

The Bloom

Forever the person who would never have to
choose

But she did

She did and she choose herslf

But this didn't mean that she had abandon in
mind

The same way it didn't mean that it was a trick
of time

Long gone is the person you met

But if the person I am not isn't enough

I hate to say it but I'll just be one of your

Past regrets

The Bloom

Not everything needs closure

Sometimes just letting it go is

Better

All of it might shatter to the ground, I know

But maybe one day when youre looking down
at it

The mosaic of those pieces together

Might become something beautiful of the past

A souvenir of the strength it took

In not allowing to lose yourself

Trying to repair

What wanted to be destroyed

— — — — — — —

The Bloom

The Bloom

Spring

The Bloom

The Bloom

Just because the moon is seen through the
reflection of the sun

Doesn't mean the sun is responsible for all the
moon has become

The way the flowers are pretty even at night

Shows that it isn't just the trick of the light

It is in the way the stars shine even when they
aren't seen

Shows that darkness didn't tell them how to be

And just because you helped me realise I had
wings to fly

Doesn't mean I became Icarus when you said
goodbye

— — — — — — —

The Bloom

I had this flowery sort of wonderful with you

The pretty essence ebbed in my head

But the petals dead

Resting in my hands

-I'd take that over plastic any day

— — — — — — —

The Bloom

I can be the painter

I can be the muse

I don't need you to

Be my inspirational blue

When I can paint the sky purple

And pink and green

Quiet well without you

———————

The Bloom

You were the sun but

I was never the moon

Your brilliance wasn't mine alone

I was a sunflower

One in many

Someone who had to strain her neck

Just to look at you clearly

But don't ever think I'd have it any other way

You were you and I was i

And there's nothing I would change

I'd rather burn in your glory

Than shine in your grace

You were the sun

And I was the sunflower

Who fell in vain

The Bloom

The Bloom

Of all the treasures that I've held

Your face was the most precious

The most beautiful

The dearest

The most heart wrenching

For when the time came

For me to let go of you

Even our goodbyes felt

Too good to be true

––––––––

The Bloom

The Bloom

These days

If a song reminds me of you

I just go to the place

You hated to

Blast the song loud and make sure you

Feel it in your bones

And know it too

Just how much I'm fazed by you

————————

The Bloom

The Bloom

I was kind with my waves

But the storm is due

I don't know if you'll make it through

I don't wish anything bad for you

But know I'll be fair

And try to drown you too

— — — — — — —

The Bloom

The Bloom

The mirror

Was never really liked by me

Because I chose to believe

What it reflected was what I was meant to see

But now I know clearly

That's not the truth

I can see whatever I want and not just what it
shows

The mirror doesn't know

All that I can be

The mirror only shows

What it sees

I just need to decide

Whether I should

The Bloom

Believe the mirror the mirror that doesn't
know me

Or believe the person who does

The person who is me

− − − − − − − −

The Bloom

Did I tell you I love you?

No?

Oh well how could i?

It seems that the words don't wish to leave my
tongue

They like to play hide and seek, you know

They like to play games with my heart and my
head

They like to render me speechless by not
letting any other word pass unless they do

And my dear, it seems like you aren't helping
much either

Because no matter how bold these words
might be when playing games

They become shy in your presence

They lose their sense of direction and end up
sitting in the farthest corner

The Bloom

Not wanting to come out

But how can I blame you?

My darling, I can't

But don't blame me too

It might take time

But I'll try my best to trick these words out of
my mouth

So that one day they won't be shy anymore

And let me scream at the top of my lungs

Just how much I love you

— — — — — — —

The Bloom

I counted my life in ashes

Now see me rise in flame

I swam every ocean

Now see me in the waves

I was flying high

I was touching moonlight

I was in every earthquake that made my fears
cry

It was in every one of my smiles

The Bloom

The Bloom

You can speak nonsense

Know that I'll understand

Just let me into your head for a while

Is it beautiful in there as I imagine it to be

For all I know there's beauty in there of infinity

You can say all you want, I won't mind

Every piece of you I crave

No matter how jaggedly undefined

\- - - - - - -

The Bloom

I will eat the entire sky

Sun included

And watch as you look at me, fascinated

Of the glow on my skin

The brilliance in my eyes

I will

Rise from ashes

Not the ashes which signified my end

To you

But the ashes wherein my true form was
planted

Wherein my true self grew

The Bloom

Revenge burnt a stamp on my skin

Stained my cheeks red

Made my tongue dry

But why did all of it change

When I saw your smile

The sky turned blue

Oh and how wonderful too

My heart beat slowed

With peace and growth

_ _ _ _ _ _ _

The Bloom

It gets better

I swear it does

And when it will, you will realise

That you believing that it will

Is what made it better

It wasn't some fairy godmother with her wand
and magic

It was you with your passion and will

It was you who got your hands dirty

Who built a castle for yourself

Not a castle of sand which built itself and
destroyed itself too

But a house you would call home

A castle where you would grow

— — — — — — —

The Bloom

I'm dancing with autumn

I don't hate her no more

She doesn't make me sad like before

The fallen leaves she leaves at my doorstep
don't

Make me bleed anymore

She taught me to get through even if I fall

And how wonderful it is after all

I'm dancing with autumn while she steps on my
toes

Giving me a smile

Like that of a child who stole

– – – – – – – –

The Bloom

 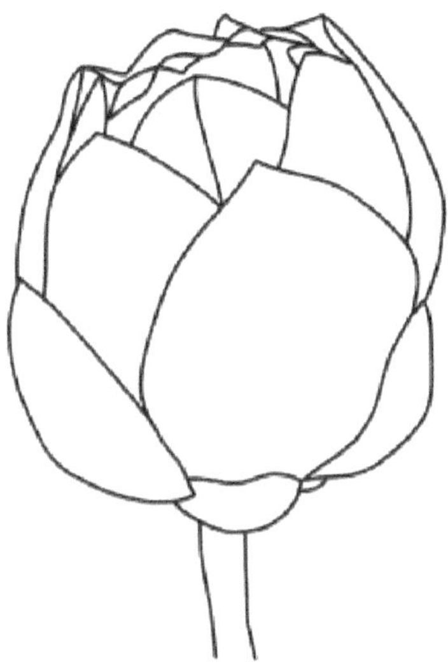

The Bloom

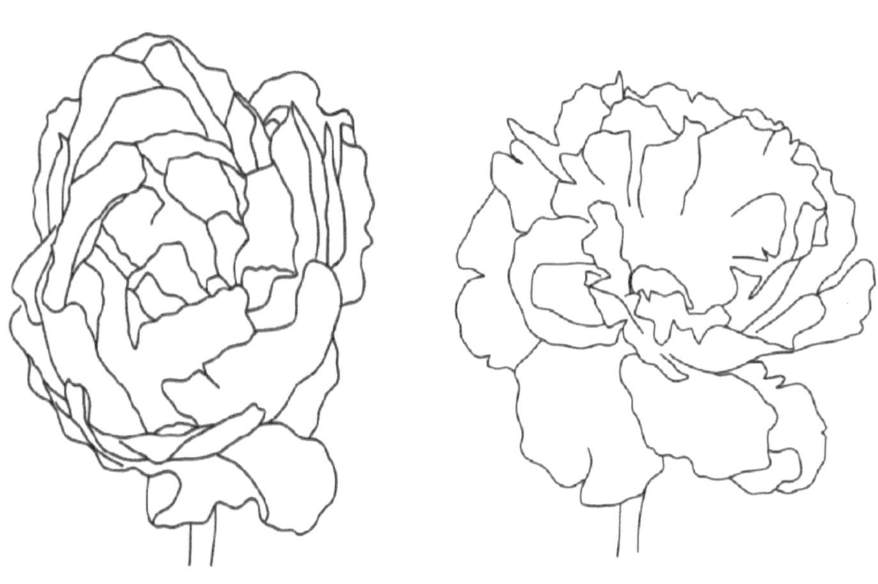

The Bloom

The End

www.ingramcontent.com/pod-product-compliance
Lightning Source LLC
Chambersburg PA
CBHW031751150726
47989CB00006B/2667